TICKET

LITTLE LEAGUE
WORLD SERIES

MARTIN GITLIN

ADMIT ONE — THE BIG GAME — YOUR FRONT ROW SEAT

45th Parallel Press

Published in the United States of America by Cherry Lake Publishing Group
Ann Arbor, Michigan
www.cherrylakepublishing.com

Reading Adviser: Beth Walker Gambro, MS Ed., Reading Consultant, Yorkville, IL.

Photo Credits: © AP Photo/Gene J. Puskar, cover; © Farid Studio/Shutterstock, inside cover, 13, 19, 25, 29; © Nosyrevy/Shutterstock, 2, 3, 6, 10, 16, 23, 32; © tammykayphoto/Shutterstock, 5; © AP Photo/Gene J. Puskar/ASSOCIATED PRESS, 7; From the collection of the Lycoming County Historical Society and Thomas T. Taber Museum, 9; Columbus Metropolitan Library, Public domain, via Wikimedia Commons, 11; Jenny Fulle (Copyright holder), CC BY-SA 3.0 via Wikimedia Commons, 12; Courtesy of Indiana State Library, 15 (top); © Dylanhatfield/Shutterstock, 15 (bottom); © AP Photo/Charlie Riedel/ASSOCIATED PRESS, 17; © AP Photo/G. Paul Burnett/ASSOCIATED PRESS, 18; © AP Photo/Gene J. Puskar, File/ASSOCIATED PRESS, 21; © PeopleImages.com - Yuri A/Shutterstock , 22; © AP Photo/Tom E. Puskar/ASSOCIATED PRESS, 24; By Sports Service - Public Domain via Wikimedia Commons, 27; Keith Allison from Baltimore, USA, CC BY-SA 2.0 via Wikimedia Commons, 27; © Keeton Gale/Shutterstock, 28

Copyright © 2026 by Cherry Lake Publishing Group

All rights reserved. No part of this book may be reproduced or utilized in any form or by any means without written permission from the publisher.

45th Parallel Press is an imprint of Cherry Lake Publishing Group.

Library of Congress Cataloging-in-Publication Data

Names: Gitlin, Marty, author.
Title: Ticket to the Little League World Series / by Martin Gitlin.
Description: Ann Arbor, Michigan : 45th Parallel Press, [2025] | Series: The Big Game | ATOS: 3.5. | Incudes bibliographical references. | Audience: Grades 7-9 | Summary: "Who has won the Little League World Series? How did they make it happen? Filled with high-interest text written with struggling readers in mind, this series includes fun facts, intriguing stories, and captivating play-by-plays from the World Series of Little League"-- Provided by publisher.
Identifiers: LCCN 2025009136 | ISBN 9781668963876 (hardcover) | ISBN 9781668965191 (paperback) | ISBN 9781668966808 (ebook) | ISBN 9781668968413 (pdf)
Subjects: LCSH: Little League World Series (Baseball)--History--Juvenile literature. | Little league baseball--Pennsylvania--History--Juvenile literature. | Little League Baseball (Organization)--Juvenile literature.
Classification: LCC GV880.5 .G58 2025 | DDC 796.357/620974851--dc23/eng/20250508
LC record available at https://lccn.loc.gov/2025009136

Cherry Lake Publishing Group would like to acknowledge the work of the Partnership for 21st Century Learning, a Network of Battelle for Kids. Please visit Battelle for Kids online for more information.

Printed in the United States of America

Note from publisher: Websites change regularly, and their future contents are outside of our control. Supervise children when conducting any recommended online searches for extended learning opportunities.

Table of Contents

Introduction 4
History of the Game 8
Early Days, Big Moments 14
Modern Moments 20
All-stars of the Game 26

    ACTIVITY 30
    LEARN MORE 30
    GLOSSARY 31
    INDEX 32
    ABOUT THE AUTHOR 32

Introduction

Players adjust their stance. Cleats scrape the ground. Dust rises off the field. Hands flex in mitts. Fielders get low. They watch the batter. The pitcher winds up. The game is on!

Millions of kids play baseball. They play in parks. They play in fields. They play in streets. Most just want to have fun. They try to win. But the score is not important.

That is mostly true in Little League. It is **organized** baseball. Organized means ordered or structured. Little League is organized into smaller leagues. Each league has many teams. And every team has many players.

The waiting is over and the big game is about to begin. Get ready, Little League fans!

Winning is important to some. They play to win a **championship**. That is an event that decides the league winner. Some try to reach the Little League World Series. That is an **annual** event. It is played every year. The Series is held in Williamsport, Pennsylvania.

The event is not just for U.S. teams. Teams come from all over the world. International teams compete against each other. So do U.S. teams. Then the winners play for the title.

Fans fill the stadium. They watch on TV. Millions of people tune in. The next generation of baseball is taking the field.

Let the big game begin!

James Feliciano celebrates his Lake Mary, Florida, team's Little League World Series win in 2024.

History of the Game

It was 1938. Carl Stotz had an idea. He lived in Williamsport. Stotz had no sons. He played baseball with his nephews. Stotz wanted more local kids involved. He brought them together.

Stotz soon took the next step. He started a baseball group. Stotz called it Little League. He reached out to businesses. They were **sponsors**. That means they gave money to support the teams. They paid for baseball equipment and uniforms. Teams wore the sponsoring business's names on their jerseys. Teams were named after their sponsor.

Carl Stotz is pictured here with two Lycoming Dairy team members.

The first game was June 6, 1939. Lundy Lumber beat Lycoming Dairy. The score was 23–8. But Lycoming Dairy got another chance. It later beat Lundy Lumber for the first championship.

Little League grew slowly. Its first World Series was in 1947. Every team was from Pennsylvania or New Jersey. A team from Williamsport, Pennsylvania, won.

Back then, there were only 48 states. Little League was soon in all of them. Youth baseball became popular in other nations, too. Among them was Canada. It was the first country to join the Series. Its Montreal team was added in 1952.

American teams kept winning the Series. Their run ended in 1957 and 1958. That was when Mexico won. They had just joined that year. But the United States continued to dominate. No international team would win again until 1967.

A Little League game in Hartford Park, Worthington, Ohio, in the 1950s

Japan was added in 1961. Japan won the event in 1967 and 1968. Taiwan joined in 1969. It took 4 straight titles. It won those 4 games by a combined score of 42–4.

That embarrassed American officials. They banned international teams in 1975. That move upset other countries. They were allowed to return in 1976. Then Japan or Taiwan won every Series from 1976 to 1981.

The event kept growing. A total of 29 countries have competed. So have 44 U.S. states. And it has not been limited to boys. A total of 23 girls have also played.

Jenny Fulle (at bat) was the first girl to officially play for a Little League team in the U.S. in 1974.

A team from Mexico arrived in 1957. Its players were small. They averaged 92 pounds (41.7 kilograms). Nobody expected them to win. But they did.

One reason was Angel Macias. He could pitch left-handed. He could pitch right-handed. He led his team to the championship game.

Then he did something special. Macias pitched a perfect game. He allowed no hitter to reach base. Macias struck out 11 batters.

U.S. teams had always won the Little League World Series. Macias ended that streak on that day. His team from Mexico had become the first. There would be many more to follow.

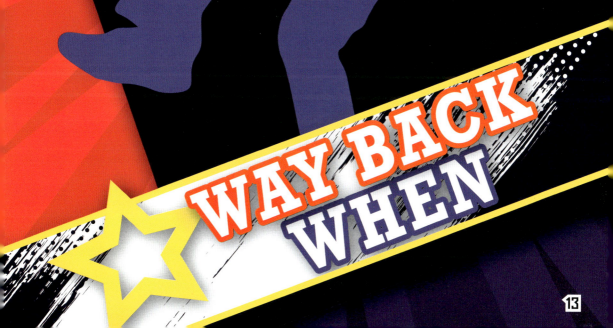

WAY BACK WHEN

Early Days, Big Moments

Lloyd McClendon played in the Major Leagues. McClendon was an outfielder. This position plays in the grass outside of the infield. He played for 8 years. McClendon played mostly with the Pittsburgh Pirates.

He later became a **manager** of the same team. A manager makes many decisions. He decides which players to put on the field.

But McClendon was a Little League World Series star first. It was 1971. McClendon was 12 years old. He was playing for a team from Gary, Indiana.

This team was the first all-Black team to compete. McClendon was its youngest player. He was nervous. But he was about to do something special.

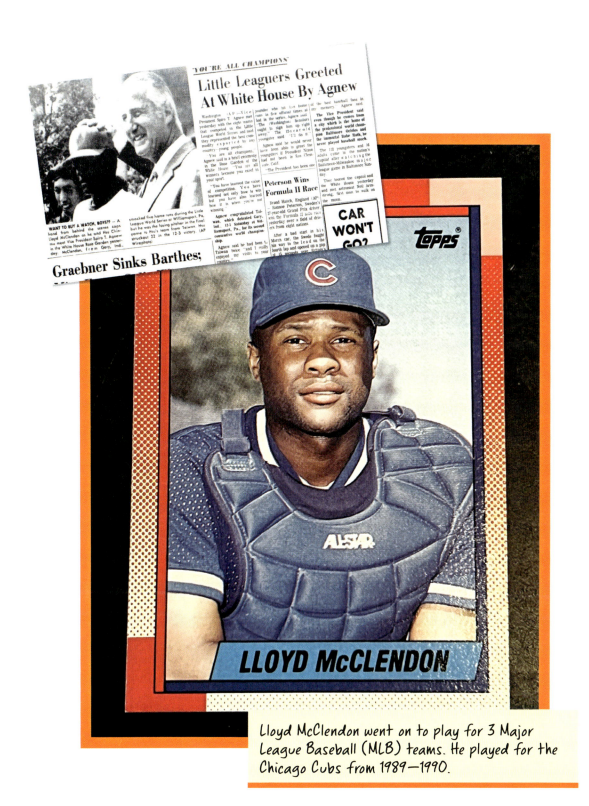

Lloyd McClendon went on to play for 3 Major League Baseball (MLB) teams. He played for the Chicago Cubs from 1989—1990.

It was August 25, 1971. The Indiana team needed to beat Kentucky. But Indiana had something Kentucky did not. It had McClendon. He hit a home run. Then he hit another. He was the star of the game. Indiana won, 7–2.

But McClendon's team needed 2 more wins to take the title. McClendon was not done playing hero. His next win was against a team from Spain. He beat Spain with 2 more home runs.

Beating Taiwan would make Indiana the champion. McClendon swung at the first pitch he saw. And he hit a fifth home run!

He came to bat 3 more times. But he never saw another pitch. Taiwan walked him each time. That was a good idea. Taiwan won the game. And it took the Series title.

Eleven years later, Taiwan was dominating. It was 1982. It seemed Taiwan would never lose. Its teams won 5 Series straight. It was about to win another. Taiwan had won 31 games in a row. And it had reached the finals again.

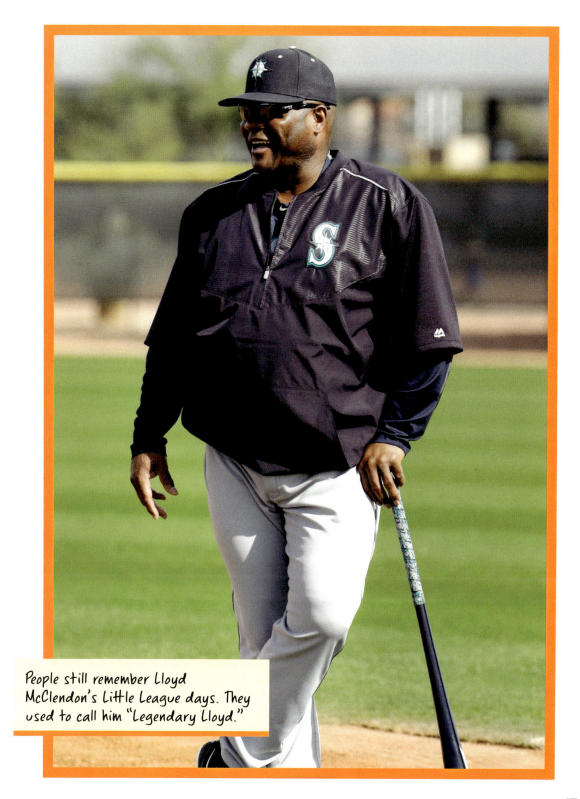

People still remember Lloyd McClendon's Little League days. They used to call him "Legendary Lloyd."

One opponent stood in Taiwan's way. That was a team from Kirkland, Washington. The stands were packed with 40,000 fans. Some believed Kirkland had no chance.

But Kirkland believed in itself. Its pitcher was Cody Webster. Webster threw fast pitches. He even had a **curveball**. It curves down as it reaches the plate. Webster allowed just 2 hits to Taiwan. The result was a 6-0 Kirkland victory.

Kirkland pitcher Cody Webster threw the first pitch at a New York Mets game. This was right after Kirkland's Little League win over Taiwan.

Batters could not hit balls pitched by Danny Almonte. He pitched for the Bronx, New York. It appeared he would pitch the Bronx to the 2001 title. First, Almonte threw a no-hitter. He followed that with a perfect game. That means no hits and no walks. No one on the other team got on base.

The Bronx finally lost in the U.S. finals. Almonte did not pitch that game. But something else was wrong. People began to wonder. Little League players could not be older than 12. Almonte looked older.

They were right. They checked his age. They were shocked. Almonte was 14. He had cheated. So had his team. The Bronx had to **forfeit** its wins. This means to give up a win for wrongdoing.

Modern Moments

The Series has had 23 players that were girls. But there was only one Mo'ne Davis. Davis was among Little League's best pitchers ever.

Davis pitched for the Taney Dragons in 2014. That team was from Pennsylvania. She pitched the ball at 70 miles (112.7 kilometers) per hour. That is very fast. Davis also threw a curveball. It was nearly impossible to hit.

Davis pitched a **shutout** against the team from Nashville, Tennessee. This means she did not allow a run. Davis struck out 8 batters. Millions watched her pitch her next game on TV. Her team lost that game. But she had made history.

Mo'ne Davis made a huge splash as a pitcher.

There have been over 70 grand slams in the history of the Little League World Series.

Davis isn't the only player who had a big moment. A player from Hollywood did, too. Hollywood is a neighborhood in Los Angeles, California. It is where TV shows and movies are filmed. Hollywood is not famous for baseball. But it was in 2023. A Little League team made sure of it. That team was El Segundo.

El Segundo was not supposed to win. But it reached the Series final against Curaçao. El Segundo led 5–1. It was the fifth inning. Then Curaçao player Nasir El-Ossais hit a **grand slam**. That is a home run with 3 runners on base. It scores 4 runs. The game was tied at 5–5.

Soon Louis Lappe came to bat. He was an El Segundo standout. He had already hit 4 home runs in the Series. And he blasted another. It soared over the fence. Lappe flipped his bat in the air. He wanted to celebrate. So did his teammates. They had a party on the field.

The next year, a team from Florida had a shot at the title. It was 2024. Lathan Norton played on the Florida team. But he was sick. He had a bad fever. He was too sick to play that Saturday. Norton got better on Sunday. That was lucky. Because he was about to be a hero.

Lathan Norton, number 18, celebrates with his team after their 2024 win.

Florida was playing Taiwan. The title was on the line. The score was tied at 1–1. It was the eighth inning. Norton was on second base. His teammate Hunter Alexander **bunted**. That is when a batter does not swing the bat. Instead, the batter holds the bat across home plate. The bat hits the ball into the dirt. It can help move a runner to the next base.

A Taiwan player picked up the ball. He threw it badly. Norton sprinted around third base. Then he scored. Florida had the winning run. And it had the championship.

The best player to emerge from the Series? It might have been Gary Sheffield. He played for Tampa, Florida, in 1980. Sheffield was a pitcher and hitter. He became only a hitter in the Major Leagues.

Sheffield sure could hit as a kid. He hit .600 in the Little League World Series. That means he averaged 3 hits in every 5 at-bats. He helped his team beat Rhode Island and Washington.

Sheffield played for 22 seasons. He hit 509 home runs. He made 9 all-star teams.

All-stars of the Game

Little League All-stars may go on to greatness. Some become baseball legends.

John Powell

John Powell is a baseball legend. His nickname was Boog. He played in the 1954 Little League World Series. His team was from Lakeland, Florida.

He went on to play in the MLB. Pitchers hated him there. He beat them with home runs. Powell was an amazing slugger. He hit 339 home runs. His team was the Baltimore Orioles. Powell played nearly his entire career with Baltimore.

John "Boog" Powell in 1966

JOHN POWELL, Orioles

Powell threw the first pitch for an Orioles game on his 80th birthday in 2021.

Cody Bellinger

Cody Bellinger was another Little League player who went on to the Major League. He played in the 2007 Little League World Series. His team was Chandler, Arizona. He got 3 hits in one game. One was a home run. Bellinger said it was the most fun he ever had playing baseball.

That is saying a lot. Bellinger became a Major League star. He won the Rookie of the Year award in 2017. That is given to the best first-year player. He was playing for the Los Angeles Dodgers. He now makes big money. But he still says Little League was more fun.

Bellinger played for the Los Angeles Dodgers from 2017 to 2022.

Ed Vosberg, Jason Varitek, and Michael Conforto all played in 3 World Series. There are 3 levels of World Series. First is the Little League World Series. Second is the College World Series. Finally, there is the Major League World Series. Only 3 players have played in all 3 World Series.

★ Ed Vosberg competed for Tucson, Arizona, in 1973. Then he played for the University of Arizona in 1980. He played for the champion Florida Marlins in 1997.

★ Jason Varitek was on a Florida team. It was in the 1984 Little League World Series. His Georgia Tech team played for the college title in 1995. Varitek played for the majors title with the Boston Red Sox in 2004 and 2007.

★ Michael Conforto competed for a Little League team in Washington. He played college ball at Oregon. Then he was with the New York Mets in the 2015 Major League World Series.

A BIT OF TRIVIA!

Activity

Organize your own baseball game. Talk to your friends. Ask family members. Find a field to play on. You need at least 12 players.

You will also need equipment. Find out who has bats and balls at home. There are options if you cannot find enough. Ask an adult or local baseball coach. Perhaps everyone can pitch in a little money. Then use it to buy equipment. Balls and bats last a long time. You can use them for future games.

Baseball is fun. Not all games have to be Little League. They don't have to be organized by adults. Just know the rules of the game. Research how it is played. Then have fun!

Learn More

BOOKS

Johnson, Sean. *Little League World Series.* La Jolla, CA: Scobre Educational, 2015.

Ogurcak, Janice L. *The World of Little League.* Charleston, SC: Arcadia Publishing, 2015.

WEBSITES

Search these online sources with an adult.

Little League | History of Little League

Little League® World Series website

Sports Illustrated for Kids | Baseball

Glossary

annual (AN-yoo-wuhl) once a year

bunted (BUHNT-id) hit softly by a batter to move a runner forward by a base

championship (CHAM-pee-uhn-ship) event that determines the winner in a league or sport

curveball (KUHRV-bawl) pitch that curves downward

forfeit (FOR-fuht) give up a victory for wrongdoing

grand slam (GRAND SLAM) home run with 3 runners on base; it scores 4 runs

manager (MAA-nih-juhr) leader of a baseball team who makes decisions

organized (OR-guh-niyzd) planned or structured

shutout (SHUHT-owt) game where one team fails to score

sponsors (SPAHN-suhrs) businesses that pay for equipment and uniforms

Index

A
activities, 30
ages of players, 13–14, 20
all-Black teams, 14, 16
Almonte, Danny, 13
American teams, 4–6, 10, 12, 16, 18, 23–24
Arizona teams, 28–29

B
baseball
    managers, 14, 16–17
    players, 5, 7, 9, 12–16, 18–21, 23–30
    popularity, 4–6, 10, 30
    professional, 14–15, 17–18, 22, 25–29
Bellinger, Cody, 28

C
California teams, 23
Canadian teams, 11
cheating, 13
Conforto, Michael, 29
Curaçao teams, 23

D
Davis, Mo'ne, 20–21

F
Florida teams, 7, 24–26, 29
Fulle, Jenny, 12
fun, 4–6, 28, 30

G
girls in the Series, 12, 20–21

H
hitting, 11–12, 16, 22–23, 25–26, 28
home runs, 16, 22–23, 26, 28

I
Indiana teams, 14–16
international teams, 6, 11–12, 16, 18–19, 23–24

J
Japanese teams, 12

K
Kentucky teams, 16

L
Lappe, Louis, 23
Little League, 6, 30
    history, 8–12, 14
    World Series, 6–7, 10, 12–16, 18–21, 23–26, 28–29

M
Macias, Angel, 19
Major League Baseball, 14–15, 17–18, 22, 25–29
managers, 14, 16–17

McClendon, Lloyd, 14–15
Mexican teams, 10, 19

N
New Jersey teams, 10
New York teams, 13
Norton, Lathan, 23–24

P
Pennsylvania teams, 8–12, 20–21
pitchers, 5, 13, 18–21, 25–27
Powell, John "Boog," 25–27

S
Sheffield, Gary, 25
Stotz, Carl, 8–9

T
Taiwanese teams, 12, 16, 18, 24

V
Varitek, Jason, 29
Vosberg, Ed, 29

W
Washington teams, 18, 29
Webster, Cody, 18
Williamsport, Pennsylvania, 6, 8–12

About the Author

Martin Gitlin is an educational book author based in Connecticut. He won more than 45 awards as a newspaper sportswriter from 1991 to 2002. Included was a first-place award from the Associated Press for his coverage of the 1995 World Series. He has had more than 200 books published since 2006. Most of them were written for students.